Blackbeard's Treasure

ALAN PARR

A mathematical adventure for KS2

IM
IMAGINATIVE
MINDS   Imaginative Minds Ltd © 2008

Published by
Imaginative Minds Ltd © 2008

ISBN 978-1-904806-29-5

Edited by Brian Asbury
Design & production by Al Stewart
Illustration by Pat Murray

Contents

Introduction

Blackbeard's Treasure is a mathematical adventure game suitable for pupils working at Key Stage 2 of the National Curriculum. Adventure games of this kind have lots of positive features, but their advantages can be summarised as follows:

❖ *For the teacher, they are cheap and easy to administer. They also offer plentiful opportunities to observe children as they go about solving problems.*

❖ *For children, they are enjoyable and tremendously motivating. Frequently - and this tends to be particularly true of low achievers - pupils work on them with commitment, perseverance and achievement well beyond their normal levels of performance.*

A further advantage is that they meet all the specifications of OFSTED and the like - even that daunting section of 'Non-statutory guidance' which mentions words like 'fascination', 'motivation', 'pleasure' and 'enjoyment'.

What is an adventure game?

A mathematical adventure game has many of the desirable features of computer-based adventures. Most notable is the fact that all the activities are linked by a common theme and an overall problem which the children are trying to solve - perhaps they're trying to escape from a giant's castle, or explore a desert island.

However, they have a number of advantages over computer adventure games. To start with, there's the obvious fact that no computer is necessary, nor any other special equipment apart from that which is normally to be found in any classroom. Also, unlike most computer-based adventures, the tasks here can be attempted in any order, so no pupils need worry about getting held up simply because there's one problem they haven't yet been able to solve. Neither is any special expertise needed from the teacher - indeed, it is often a good idea to invite a parent or other adult to do the actual administration, so that the teacher can concentrate entirely upon observing just how the children go about tackling problems.

The story around which the adventure is built is often a very simple one. The children are given a number of problems to solve which relate to the story. This particular

adventure has eight problems which the children work on in pairs. The tasks are carefully designed so they can be presented in written form. Having two copies of each is enough for classes of up to about 30 or 32.

Each problem has a range of possible answers, and each answer brings with it a piece of information. Only when all the tasks have been finished can this accumulated information be interpreted and used to solve a final overall problem. The snippets of information can be obtained in any order, so there's no need (unless you really want to) for each one to be checked before they move on to finding the next - hence the ease of administration. Of course, correct information comes only from correct answers, so, if they have any wrong answers at all, children will not be able to solve the overall problem. This need to be 100% correct serves only to increase their motivation; contrast this with a more traditional lesson, where an 80% success rate may be seen as a good performance.

The target time for the whole process is about 90-120 minutes, but extension and follow-up activities can be devised for the early finishers and most children are happy to continue for considerably longer. Completion of the adventure is recognised by awarding the children a certificate of achievement.

Surely there must be some disadvantages to these wonderful adventures? Well, they can take a lot of thinking up; but that's really the author's problem rather than yours. There is also a certain amount of photocopying and other preparation to do, but this should take no more than an hour or so, and most of it can be done by a parent helper.

Some of this probably sounds hugely mystifying so far but, in practice, teachers and pupils assure me that the adventures are easy to use and that they *do* meet all the aims I try to build in. For example, one of my previous adventures, *S.A.-N.T.A. C.L.A.U.S.*, appeared in *Strategies* magazine's Christmas 1995 edition (Vol. 6, No. 1). Among the comments it attracted were the following:

❖ *'No special equipment was needed, the instructions were clear and my preparation was minimal.'*

❖ *'Thank you! It was fascinating to see the different approaches to the problems.'*

❖ *'The children enjoyed it immensely, becoming more and more engrossed as they tackled each activity. They begged me to "Make up another one, Miss".'*

On the trail of Blackbeard

'Blackbeard's Treasure' was originally presented in issues 1-3 of *QMS* magazine after being trialled extensively with Year 5 and Year 6 classes. The theme relates to pirates and treasure islands around 1700-1720, when piracy in the Caribbean was at its height. The material comprising the adventure consists of:

* *Eight worksheets (pp.12-13 and 16-21). You'll need to make two or three photocopies of each - it is recommended that you use punched pocket files both to make the copies more robust and to make storage easier (it should be possible to store the entire adventure in an ordinary ring binder).*

* *Two sheets of accompanying information cards (pp. 14-15), which are needed for Task 2 ('Hiring the Crew'). These will also need to be copied and the copies cut into separate cards, which should be stored with the worksheet.*

* *A two-page answer grid (pp. 22-23) to which pupils will need to refer after completing each task. These contain information for all eight problems (you'll need to make enough photocopies for each pair to have a set).*

* *The final problem sheet (p. 24 - again, each pair will need a copy). This is also the record sheet on which pupils record the information they get from the answer grids.*

* *An award certificate (p. 25) - one copy needed for each pupil.*

The adventure does not require any special equipment, nor any special classroom arrangements.

Introducing the adventure

The scene can be set by relating the story, 'The Old Man's Legacy' (p. 11), and by asking the children to 'think' themselves back in time to about the year 1720. This is, of course, an important part of the whole process; it establishes the context and it allows the atmosphere to build . The teacher can feed in some relevant background material and drop a few hints about what's in store - in the process, of course, gaining some indication of how much knowledge the children already possess.

During the course of telling the story, you should be able to bring out all the procedural points of which the children should be aware. Here's a checklist:

1. *The children will be working in pairs, or whatever other groups you decide upon. My personal requirement is simply that pairs should be compatible and have a basic reading ability, but I've worked with teachers who like to group on other criteria, and I know of one teacher who chose to use groups of four to develop team building (and very successfully, at that).*

2. *They'll be tackling eight tasks during the adventure, which relate to the different phases of the story - setting up the expedition, the voyage, and searching for the treasure. However, the tasks can be done in any order.*

3. *There is never any need to write on the instruction task sheets themselves.*

4. *Each task has several possible answers and, whenever a task is completed the children should note down the correct answer and its associated piece of information from the answer grid, which should also be written in the correct space on the record/final problem sheet.*

5. *After each task, pupils simply move onto another one - there is no need to check with the teacher.*

6. *Most of the tasks are tricky and it's easy to go wrong, so it's better if children take their time. When they've done all the eight tasks, they'll be able to tackle the final challenge, which should bring the adventure to a successful conclusion. In order to do this, they will need to have carried out every one of the previous eight tasks successfully.*

7. *It's not a race (and on the basis of previous experience, I can almost guarantee that the first pairs to finish will have got at least a couple of tasks wrong).*

Teachers' notes

The tasks which comprise this adventure are numbered 1 to 8. These numbers, however, refer to their position within the story rather than the order in which children need to tackle them. They can be attempted in any order. Notes relating to each of the tasks follow:

Task 1 – Buying your ship

If you were to come across this task in the pages of a text book, you probably wouldn't regard it as anything other than exceptionally boring practice material, but it is just one good example of how the context engenders a high level of motivation and commitment.

A task like this can also be a wonderful source of information about children's methods of working with numbers. How much of the working gets done on paper, and how much in the head? Do the methods of manipulating numbers bear any relation to conventional procedures? What short cuts do the children call upon? Can any of the possible answers be dismissed immediately? Is a calculator used? By whom? How?

In fact, this problem can be used as an assessment exercise in its own right. The correct answer is **plan B**, which the children have to note down on the appropriate section of their record sheet. The corresponding number in the second column on the answer grid is 5; they'll need to use this number later on, but at the moment its significance will not be clear. It may be helpful to emphasise that this number is not a score.

You'll note that the number which they have obtained as a result of getting the correct answer is the lowest number on the answer grid. In fact, this is the case for all eight tasks, which will make it easy for you to tell how well a pair is doing simply by glancing at their record sheet.

Task 2 – Hiring crew

This task is the only one of the eight which requires separate information sheets (pp. 14-15), which need to be photocopied and cut into constituent sections. These should be kept with the task sheet.

Mathematically, the problem is an exercise in data handling. However, of all the tasks in the adventure, this is perhaps the one which offers the most opportunity for capitalising upon the cross-curricular potential of the theme. The sheet gives information about twenty possible crew members. Every one of the names on the cards, including the females, is that of someone who was involved in piracy - mostly, though not invariably, in the Caribbean region in the period 1680-1725.

No attempt has been made to match the characteristics on the cards to the real historical figures, but there's plenty of potential to be found in deciding why these characteristics were useful ones. For example, there's the gruesome fact that the ship's carpenter might operate (*literally!*) as the ship's surgeon as well.

Of the 20 cards, **nine people** meet all the criteria given in the task for selection as crew members.

Task 3 – The crew's outfits

This challenge relates to kitting out the crew. When shillings and old pence disappeared from our lives in 1971, the parents of today's primary pupils were just about the age their children are today, so it's not surprising that today's children have virtually no knowledge of old money. This makes this task an interesting one to offer; the children will not have been taught any rules for working with shillings and pence, so the problem becomes a fresh one to be thought out from the initial concepts.

To those of us who remember shillings and pence all too well (not to mention ha'pennies and even farthings), it can seem strange when one of today's children prefers to work in decimals to handle this task. Since the purpose of the whole adventure is to offer challenges which call upon problem-solving skills, however, we can hardly complain when children use a wholly logical method simply because it seems unusual to us.

The answer here is that **two** of the outfits on the sheet are too expensive.

Task 4 – The secret code

I've always considered codes and ciphers to be rich sources of stimuli, and one day I may get around to making them a focus for an entire adventure. Their use in this particular task is really an excuse to give children some tables practice, but it has one unusual feature, in that the children will need to continue their six times table as far as 21 x 6.

As an extension activity, this provides an opportunity to look at patterns within the six times table in greater detail than is usually possible - for example, in the sequence traced out by the 'units' digit. It also shouldn't take much prompting to persuade children to choose a table of their own in order to encipher some messages for each other to tackle.

The message says, incidentally: **'There is treasure buried on Crab Island'**.

Task 5 – The ship's log

As you'd expect from the theme, there are several problems in the adventure which are built around maps, and thus are tasks which can provide potential links with the geography curriculum. This problem is chiefly concerned with compass directions, but it also presents an opportunity to get children to think about ideas relating to scale and proportion. In common with several of the tasks in this adventure, the idea behind this one may seem far-fetched, but it is actually based on reality. When Columbus made his famous journey in 1492, he found himself forced to keep a false log to show to mutinous crew members, while he kept the genuine log (which admitted how totally lost he was!) very much to himself.

The correct answer is **Page 4**. Incidentally, I suspect that geographers would want to issue a 'health warning' with this problem, since the distances involved are so large that issues arise relating to the curvature of the earth and the difficulty of representing a curved surface on a flat map.

Task 6 – Which island?

This task is another which involves maps, this time bringing in ideas relating to scale, proportion and methods of measurement. It's not the sort of problem which 10-year-olds are likely to be familiar with; however, while that might possibly disconcert them in a normal situation, it's unlikely to bother them here - they'll just go ahead and tackle it anyway! It's worth watching out for the different techniques which pupils are likely to employ - rulers, finger widths, pencils, etc. And just how do you go about measuring 5 miles when the scale only goes up to 3?

The correct island is, of course, E.

Task 7 – Exploring the island

This task is designed around the idea of envisaging what a scene looks like from different viewpoints. While this is a theme that receives very little attention in commercial maths schemes, it's worth pointing out that the 1996 Key Stage 2 tests included an example (the very first question in the extension paper) in which children were given a model made from ten cubes and asked to visualise what it looked like from different positions. As well as devising similar questions with models made from cubes and other geometric shapes, teachers can call upon scenes both inside and outside the classroom to develop and practise such skills.

The answer, by the way, is that Blackbeard was viewing the scene from **Queen's Ridge**.

Task 8 – Sharing out the gold

From the point of view of the story, this is the final task, although it does not have to be the last one attempted (since the order does not really matter, the children could tackle this one first, third or at any other point in the proceedings).

It is another of those activities that seem rather contrived at first glance, but which has a real basis in fact. Unlike the Royal Navy or merchant shipping of the time, pirate crews often displayed a remarkable degree of democracy in their organisation. Officers might be elected by a vote of all crew members, and ships would often have written agreements to which everyone was a party. These articles of

agreement might include compensation rights in the case of injury and agreed arrangements for the distribution of any treasure which they found or captured. Typically, the captain might receive anywhere from two to six shares, with junior officers getting perhaps 1¼ or 1½ shares, and ordinary crewmen one share.

There's plenty of scope for juicy arithmetic practice here, at a level way beyond that which the National Curriculum would normally consider suitable for 11-year-olds (but I wouldn't dream of letting trivia like that get in the way of letting children explore such problems for themselves). For most of us the most appropriate way of handling the problem would be to recognise that 16 (rather than 15) shares are needed, then find a way of doing the resulting long division to end up with an answer of 150 gold coins.

Concluding the tasks

You will note that none of the eight main tasks involves the use of coordinates. Many resource books suggest inviting children to draw their own desert islands and to use coordinates to identify their features, but I decided to steer clear of work in this area in order to leave it free for the teacher to use as a follow-up activity if so desired.

You may feel quite happy to let things come to a halt at this point, but it is more satisfying to tie the whole thing together by providing the children with a reason why they have been collecting all the pieces of information. As they have progressed through the adventure, they have made a note of each answer on their record sheet and the number coded against it. Just to remind you, these answers should be easy for teachers to recognise, since the correct answer for every problem is always matched against the lowest number in the answer grid.

The final problem

As they approach the point where they have successfully completed all eight tasks, you can give the children one final problem to solve. Each of the answer numbers represents the number of days taken on that particular stage of the adventure; as their final task, they are asked to use this accumulated information to find out the date of their return (which should be **July 4th**).

On completion, the children can be presented with a certificate to reward their achievement, and this can be found on the last page after the task sheets. After all, they'll probably have merited the recognition. A nice additional activity can be to put the copies of the certificate in a folder and to hide this somewhere in the classroom. Children love searching for the folder and enjoy hiding it somewhere fresh for discovery by the next group to finish.

I hope *Blackbeard's Treasure* brings you and your pupils as much satisfaction and sheer enjoyment as it has generated in the test classes and many others.

The Old Man's Legacy

'There's an old man who lives not far away from you, and he loves to tell stories of the time when he sailed the seas with Blackbeard, the most famous and most terrible pirate of all. He tells some incredible tales, and no one knows whether any of them are really true, but they're so exciting that he's always a welcome visitor.

'But one day, you hear that he's died from the wounds he suffered long ago, and he's left all his souvenirs to you and your family. There's a seaman's chest full of bits and pieces - old coins, rusty bits of metal, tattered bits of clothing, scraps of paper - but no one apart from yourself seems very interested. As you rummage through them, though, you begin to get a feeling that some of those tales might have been true after all . . .

'Maybe, just maybe, the old-fashioned writing, the mysterious numbers, the sketchy fragments of maps, are all giving you clues to where Blackbeard's treasure can be found. There's only one thing for it - you must organise an expedition to see for yourself!

'There's an awful lot to do. You'll have to purchase a ship, hire some extra crew and kit them out. You've got to decipher coded messages, and read the maps, and find the island and decide where to dig - and if you're really lucky, you'll have the treasure to share out afterwards.'

Buying your ship

You have a choice of ways to pay for your ship.

Plan A

Make one payment of £1350

Plan C

Make 5 payments of £300

Plan D

Make 6 payments - one of £150,
one of £175, one of £200, one of £225,
one of £250, one of £275

Plan B

Make 3 payments of £415

Plan E

Make 6 payments of £224

Which is the cheapest method?

Hiring crew

You need to hire some extra sailors to join your crew.

You must reject anyone who doesn't match all of these conditions:

- ❖ age 18 or older

- ❖ has been on two or more trips

- ❖ is well behaved

- ❖ has at least two useful abilities

There are 20 sailors to choose from. Use the information cards to find how many of them you will hire to go with you.

Information sheet for Task sheet 2

Name: Henry Avery Age: 18 Trips: 1 Behaviour: good Useful Abilities: brave 1	Name: Edward Teach Age: 37 Trips: 2 Behaviour: poor Useful Abilities: arithmetic strong 6 writing
Name: Grace O'Malley Age: 25 Trips: 2 Behaviour: excellent Useful Abilities: speaks French speaks German 2	Name: Bart Roberts Age: 15 Trips: 0 Behaviour: good Useful Abilities: swimmer lookout 7
Name: John Evans Age: 32 Trips: 10 Behaviour: very good Useful Abilities: writing good swimmer 3 carpenter	Name: Mary Read Age: 21 Trips: 4 Behaviour: very good Useful Abilities: navigation strong 8 speaks Spanish
Name: Walter Kennedy Age: 14 Trips: 0 Behaviour: good Useful Abilities: climbing good eyesight 4 speaks Dutch	Name: Jack Rackham Age: 19 Trips: 3 Behaviour: bad Useful Abilities: sail mender fisherman 9
Name: Henry Morgan Age: 42 Trips: 4 Behaviour: good Useful Abilities: medical carpenter 5	Name: Anne Bonny Age: 20 Trips: 4 Behaviour: good Useful Abilities: writing brave 10 swimmer

Information sheet for Task sheet 2

(continued)

Name: Ching Shih Age: 23 Trips: 1 Behaviour: excellent Useful Abilities: none 11	Name: Alexander Selkirk Age: 46 Trips: 8 Behaviour: good Useful Abilities: strong musician 16
Name: Steed Bonnet Age: 36 Trips: 6 Behaviour: excellent Useful Abilities: cook speaks French 12	Name: Charles Vane Age: 38 Trips: 4 Behaviour: bad Useful Abilities: medical 17
Name: Edward England Age: 31 Trips: 5 Behaviour: bad Useful Abilities: strong good singer 13 good climber	Name: Howel Davis Age: 24 Trips: 1 Behaviour: good Useful Abilities: carpenter 18
Name: Thomas Tew Age: 30 Trips: 3 Behaviour: good Useful Abilities: speaks Spanish clothes maker 14	Name: William Kidd Age: 16 Trips: 1 Behaviour: very good Useful Abilities: none 19
Name: Basil Ringrose Age: 27 Trips: 6 Behaviour: very good Useful Abilities: sail maker 15	Name: Sam Bellamy Age: 41 Trips: 7 Behaviour: very good Useful Abilities: strong brave 20 gunner

The crew's outfits

A sailor needs these clothes:

shirt, trousers, scarf, boots.

You can give each sailor 3 shillings to spend on clothes (1 shilling is 12 pence).

How many of these outfits would cost **too much?**

The secret code

A message in code has some important information to tell you.

You need to know that:
    6 = a, 12 = b, 18 = c, 24 = d ... and so on

Where does the message tell you to go?

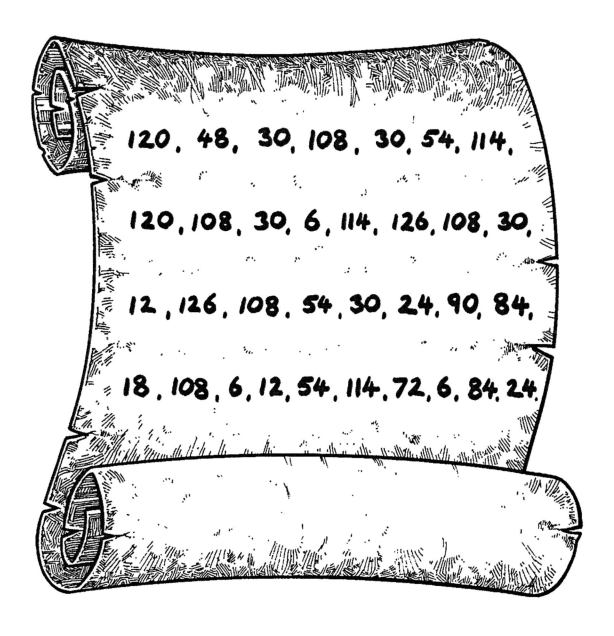

120, 48, 30, 108, 30, 54, 114,

120, 108, 30, 6, 114, 126, 108, 30,

12, 126, 108, 54, 30, 24, 90, 84,

18, 108, 6, 12, 54, 114, 72, 6, 84, 24

The ship's log

These are the pages from the ship's log for the journey from Plymouth (P) to the treasure region (T). Only one page is genuine - but which one?

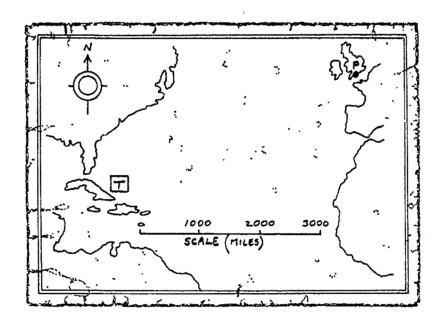

1000 miles West *then* *2000 miles North* *page 1*	*500 miles South West* *then* *2000 miles West* *then* *500 miles North West* *page 3*
2000 miles South West *then* *500 miles North* *then* *2500 miles West* *page 2*	*1500 miles West* *then* *2500 miles South West* *then* *500 miles West* *page 4*

Which island?

There are lots of little islands. Which is the one you're looking for?

Your chart tells you that the island you want is:

> 3 miles from **Marsh Island**
> 2 miles from **Old Island**
> ...and 5 miles from **Rum Island**.

Which of the small islands is the right one?

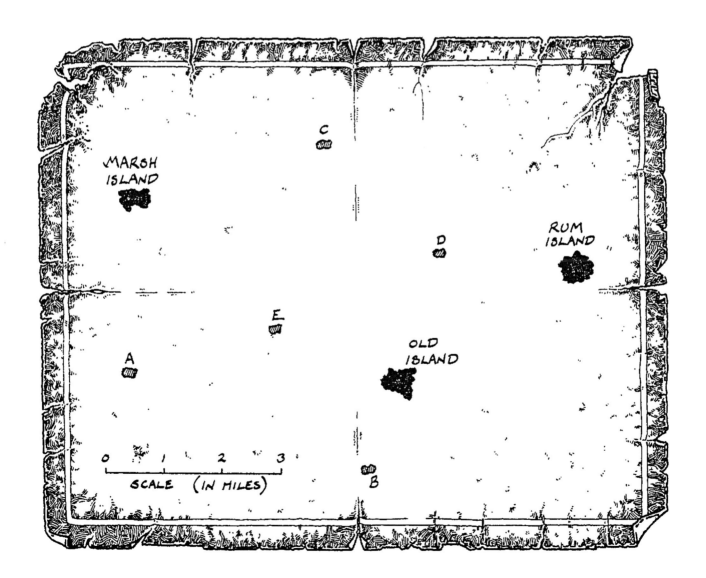

Exploring the island

There are five possible places where the treasure may be buried (they're marked ✱)

These are the clues on Blackbeard's map:

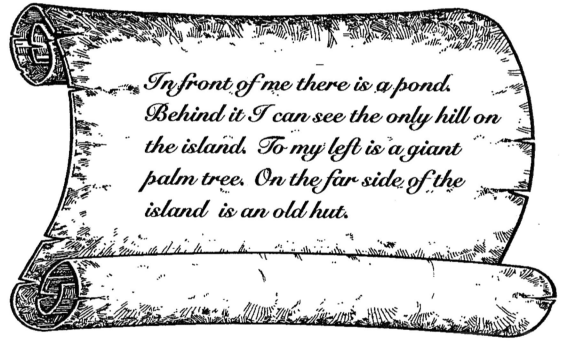

In front of me there is a pond. Behind it I can see the only hill on the island. To my left is a giant palm tree. On the far side of the island is an old hut.

Where will you dig for the treasure?

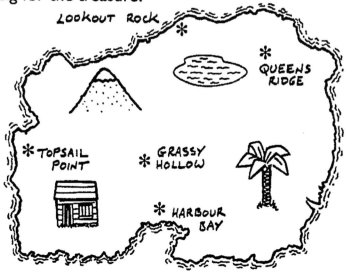

Sharing out the gold

When the treasure is counted, there are 2,400 gold coins.

Including yourself, there are 15 people in the crew.

The treasure is shared out between you, but because you are the captain you get two shares.

How much is a single share worth?

Answer grids

Task 1: BUYING YOUR SHIP

You choose payment method:

A	10
B	5
C	13
D	7
E	6

Task 2: HIRING CREW

You hire:

8 or fewer	8
9	3
10	5
11	4
12 or more	6

Task 3: THE CREW'S OUTFITS

How many outfits cost too much?

0	5
1	11
2	1
3	9
4	14
5	3

Task 4: THE SECRET CODE

You have to go to:

Caribbean	6
Crab Island	2
Mexico	8
Spain	4
West Indies	7

Answer grids continued

Task 5: THE SHIP'S LOG

The genuine page is:

Page 1	42
Page 2	47
Page 3	45
Page 4	38

Task 6: WHICH ISLAND?

The correct island is:

A	12
B	9
C	8
D	5
E	4

Task 7: EXPLORING THE ISLAND

The treasure is buried at:

Harbour Bay	9
Lookout Rock	7
Topsail Point	6
Queen's Ridge	4
Grassy Hollow	11

Task 8: SHARING OUT THE GOLD

A share is worth:

Fewer than 145 gold coins	9
Between 145 and 155	2
Between 156 and 165	5
166 or more	10

Record sheet and final problem

❖ Your answer numbers tell you how many days each part of the adventure takes you.

❖ The return journey to Plymouth takes 45 days.

❖ The first task starts on March 22nd. When do you get back to Plymouth?

	Number of days
Task 1: BUYING YOUR SHIP	
Task 2: HIRING CREW	
Task 3: THE CREW'S OUTFITS	
Task 4: THE SECRET CODE	
Task 5: THE SHIP'S LOG	
Task 6: WHICH ISLAND?	
Task 7: EXPLORING THE ISLAND	
Task 8: SHARING OUT THE GOLD	
THE RETURN JOURNEY	45

This is to certify

. . . .

has solved all the problems and has found

BLACKBEARD'S TREASURE

About the author

Alan Parr is a primary mathematics consultant and lives in Tring, Hertfordshire. He is always delighted to hear from teachers and pupils who have used one of his adventures.

Acknowledgements

My very grateful thanks are due to numerous people who have helped in all sorts of ways, including everyone who responded so favourably to previous adventures, and especially the schools who tested *Blackbeard's Treasure*. These include the pupils and teachers at St. Thomas More RC JMI, Berkhamsted, and at Little Gaddesden JMI; Harry Armitage and staff and pupils at The Rookeries Carleton J&I School, Pontefract; Rosemary Morgan and pupils at Lambs Lane CPS, Reading; Clare Neuberger and pupils; and Claire Morris, colleagues and pupils.

Thanks are also due to David Cordingly, the leading authority on pirates; to Rex Walford of the Geographical Association and much else; and to Dorothy Marsh of the City Arts Centre, Edinburgh; and to Theo Clarke for much helpful information.

Recommended reading

David Cordingly, *Life Among the Pirates:* Little, Brown & Co, ISBN 0 316 91148 8. I had to work surprisingly hard to get hold of much of the information I needed, and this book was invaluable.

David Cordingly and John Falconer, *Pirates, Fact and Fiction:* Collins and Brown, ISBN 1 85585 108 3. Both teachers and pupils will find this accessible and informative.

Clinton V. Black, *Pirates of the West Indies:* Cambridge Caribbean, ISBN 0 521 35818 3. Both cheap and authoritative.

Pirates of the Past: Hodder, ISBN 0 340 63623 8. An entertaining book for children at a pocket money price.